Thoughts that helped me to heal

Nelmin Key

Impressum

Copyright: © Nelmin Key
Jahr: 2023

ISBN: 9798861005203
Independently published

Lektorat/ Korrektorat: Abby Hale
Covergestaltung: Nelmin Key

Verlagsportal: Amazon kdp

Nelmin Avdic
c/o COCENTER
Koppoldstr. 1
86551 Aichach

Die Deutsche Nationalbibliothek verzeichnet diese Publikation in der Deutschen Nationalbibliografie.

I can't be by your side
so I am writing you this book

it's yours
my heart
my soul
my mind

This book is the key to my heart
so can you understand

How much I love you
even if I say nothing out loud

Pain in life, joy in life
healing in life
poetry, poems, songs
everything
what your soul needs to heal

What if memories that always come back
are memories from the past lives

Maybe I will never get the chance to show you my love
but your soul will always feel my love
deep inside

How long can you wait ?

a soul

can wait forever

if she

found her soulmate

Now it's all over
and you lose hope
but they keep pushing us together
when we are least expecting it

Is it hell or heaven ?

we don't know
what the universe is trying to tell us

Never let a bad start to the day

lose your hope in a good evening

it's your choice

how it ends

Carefree days make me happy
many things make me sad
be true to yourself
you can't reach 100%
of one of them
neither of the two is of eternal duration
you must find the balance

Your eyes say

that you don't love me anymore

don't lie to me about happiness

tell me honestly if your soul is still looking for me

Don't let

The

Ego

W!N

Cameras can take pictures

but eyes take memories that last forever

You

Are

Only

True

In

My

Dreams

We are counting matches on dating apps
but we can't speak
to each other in person
we have the right words
on our minds
but they never saw the
daylight

Your brown eyes

are the key to your spiritual mind

after seeing you smile

I belive butterflies can fly

you don't have to try

and you are more beautiful

with all your scars

We could be in Paris
if it had worked with us
we could watch the sunset
I know you are upset with me
but you are stubborn
like a Capricorn

Looking at your picture
looking at your smile again
and again
I know I can't turn back time
I know you will never be mine
again

Your words were so sweet

but eyes didn't lie

they will tell the truth

when you can't

and the truth is

that your words are

worthless

Driving around the world

trying to find your soul

in every beautiful eyes

I met on my way

I will never arrive

it's a road with no end

your soul is

inviolable

incomparable

unique

I am tired of my overthinking

because you told me so many times

everything was fine

I remember your blue eyes

and I sink into my overthinking again

I wish I could escape

but the water

(my own mind)

is so deep

when I freeze and focus

on it too much

I am tired of losing a part of my heart
because it hurts so hard
I close my eyes and remember yours
found hope again like a smaragd
everything is so crystal clear
you always played with my heart

So many eyes

so many souls

so much wasted time

but your hazel eyes will always be my favorite

I wish you would still care

as much as I do

I wish we could start all over

again

because I can feel it

our souls are connected

in every dimension

If I could die today

I would die yesterday

Why don't you start

why don't you let your dreams come true

I

wasn't afraid

of losing

I was afraid of

success

why don't you let your dreams come true

Happiness was invented by

the unfortunate

so they could believe

in something

after

love

I don't want to lose you
but I can't help myself
from making the same old mistakes
I would love to hold your hand
but I know I can't
must leave your hand
to keep you safe

We share our darkest secrets
we know we can keep it
we were holding out for a hero
to save our lives
from the first minute
I can't get you out of my head

*Tired of losing you
I keep losing
the only thing I always wanted was
to find someone like you
that's impossible
'cause you can't be changed*

If you give me the change

I would keep my mindset on our

future

I don't want to lose

you

the universe will keep our souls

secure

It shouldn't

scare you

to feel something

you should

be scared

of not

feeling

anything

Appearance or character

A body fades over time
merging into itself
the mind stays pure
as your age
you enjoy it and stay fit
but you've had enough
of looking perfect
why waste time on your looks
you should be focused
on your soul

Home isn't home

people who make

your life worth living

are

your

home

What if I kill myself

just

to feel something

what would happen

if you let me in

but you choose

to break me

why your heart chooses to break itself

I still love you
I still write you songs
I still breathe just for you
even if I am no longer a
lodger
in your heart

I still love you

You're still my favorite dream

black hair and hazel eyes

two souls apart, but they were one

to me, you are like no other

if I tried to describe

how much I miss you

I couldn't

you're perfectly aware of this

god connected our paths

but we've cut our luck

we turned our backs on everything

that is good for us

In love, we are stubborn

in my dreams, we still kiss

I lose you even more in daylight

we live life like a punishment

all we need is ourselves

I miss your madness

you miss my stamina

souls apart

but our hearts beat

in the same frequency

even if they are miles apart

Tell me someone loves you more
writing songs
writing poems
writing a book about us

but I am not even close
to letting you go

you are still reaching out for me
but blame me for doing the same

Fate crossed our paths
but we can't stop fighting
we don't find each other
like a puzzle
falling on the ground
we choose the wrong paths out of
stubbornness

I will wait for you forever
an end is far from sight
next time our paths cross
please don't play games
'cause I can't wait

I miss you
asking myself
what are you doing
are you smiling
or crying
chance missed

We just met
but I can say things are going pretty well
you call me from everywhere
and I am not afraid

I don't want to skip the small talk
I could have all-day long deep talks with you
all night long watching the stars
I don't want to be hurt by you
pretty sure that won't be the case, and it's the
true

going on cute dates
taking you off the streets into the moonlight
and it's all so clear
we don't lose our hearts
we found true love

our love is nothing
because nothing is perfect
you are my home now
from now to always
give you love every day

I found my home now

I tried to be someone you could love

but to be honest

I'm slowly giving up

all these years

I wasted to be like you wanted me to be

want to be free

and now you are mad at me

because I want to live my life

I guess my wounds will never heal

this pain makes me someone

I could only dream of

you think I am selfish

but how could I be

it just doesn't make sense

You break me every single day
to build me like you want me to be
but I am all alone by myself
in my own prison
I am only free in my mind
but one day, I will be free

one day
was the sixth of January
so cold outside
but I don't feel the snow
I only feel the clear air that arrives in
my mind
I am free now
and I am still here
how beautiful

I wish my little me

could see me now

we have come so far

but they still want to break us

don't say you want the best for me

when the best for me is a life without you

I was at my lowest

and you know it

and you say nothing about it

I will never forget your words

you

are

nothing

without

me

are some of them

but only the tip of the iceberg

But how could it be true

when I am free now

you said I could make nothing happen

without you

but how could it be true

I found myself

I got a dog and a house

my marriage is next week

but you are not invited

and you will never be

be missed around my little family

around my healed world

without your toxicity

why are you so scared of me

did we switch the roles

I guess I know

I became someone you could never break again

Every night I see a clear star

and I think it only shines for me

and in my wildest fantasy

I hope it's you

the lonely star on the bright heaven

and I am lonely in my bed

and doesn't feel like home

but the star gave me hope

it's shining down on me

right into my bedroom

to keep the nightmare away

and wish me

sweet dreams every night

when you are not here

And I still can't forget you

and I hope

you will forgive me

one day

because I can't trust myself

anymore

so I hope one day

the star comes down

and we met like days before

because I can't wait anymore

the reason why I still wish you

sleep well, and I hope you have sweet dreams

every night is to keep you safe

accepted there are not mine

you don't dream about me

I want to let you go

but I can't get you out of my head

you are the last thing

I think about before I go to bed

you visit me in my dreams

when I wake up, I miss you even more

because you are also the first thought

I got a book, the pages are blank

but I have so much to write

so much I had survived

demons are losing the fight

the fight I took, I can't win

but I am still here

I am still alive

no one knows my pain

my past

no one would understand

understand

why I am still fighting

I wish you would know

that you are not alone

believe me when I say

I want it all

I want it all

you ask me what I mean

I want night walks

only with you

I want to talk about your pain

I want to take it (your pain)

let's share it

I will take care of it

about your pain

you still ask me how i will survive

You will never be alone

that's not just a mood

to take you into my bed and take your virginity

I want to be your first time

and I still don't mean my

damn

fucking bed

I want to take you on trips

I want to take you to places

you've never been before

take all your pain

for the first time

let's talk all night long

I know you will never lose

you ask me how I know

what will happen in the future

I answered

together we only can win

never lose again

because you are my future

and

my life

It seems so easy for you

to play with me

one night you need me

you treat me like a wounded lamb

but the other night

you rammed a knife into the lamb

from behind

what does it mean

what should it tell me

maybe the lamb is a metaphor for me

but the real thing is

I don't know if I'm

your lover

friend

or enemy

I'm fascinated by how kind you are

but my feelings overwhelm me

every day

I see you

do you see me too

I will never know that

because I don't dare to ask you

I tremble cause I'm very afraid

of what you will say

you show me nothing

and then you show me more

I love you

but our situation tears me apart

I can feel how we're falling apart

I can't keep up our love anymore

I can't hold on anymore

when you're about to let go

I can't give anymore

when you're about to just take

You told me

now it's all over

the darkness is away, and the sun is awake

and that I had you forever

how could I have thought forever

I want to meet you

I want to hold your hand

like the first time

I don't want it to end

but you have to the brave

to choose what is better for you and me

it was us or a fucking break up

One moment

I can't live without you
but I see
you can perfectly
without me
it takes one moment
one moment
to turn my world upside down
one moment
to make me smile
one moment
to fall in love
and one moment
to break my heart

but it takes forever
to forget you

And it's raining again outside

and you are not by my side

can't hold my feelings inside

I think the drink hits too hard on me

and remember me of you

I am so tired of running

I am running away

running away from who I am

tired of being be someone else

running away from feelings

I tried to hide them deep inside

running away from people

that think they know me

but how is someone supposed to know me

when I don't know who I am

I had so much to say

but the words don't come out of my mouth

my head is full of them

I think I am losing my mind

I had so much that I wish I had said

but sometimes, it's better to hold on

to stop things before they start

how have I been so blind

you were so toxic to me

I don't care how long our love will stay
one week
one year
ten years
or
a destiny
I will always be true to you

We will never meet

I stay long nights alone in my bed

can't stop thinking about why you would leave me

at the moment, I can't think

about how to live my life without you

so it will never be complete again

but you are in my heart

so deeply

Maybe we met in a another life
but this one is pretty nice
pretty nice from the outside
but inside, I can't stop searching for you
but I am scared
would you love the face that grows out without
you
at least I forgive you
so please accept what I've become

It was hard

it wasn't fair

you threw me in the cold water

without knowing what would happen to me

I had luck

luck and unluck can't live without one

they didn't like what I've become

but I hope you will because

you were there for my first breath

will you be there in my last one

because you are the only one

just you and me

and the question, I don't know who I could ask for

Don't get me wrong
I don't want to ruin your perfect life from the
outside
I just want to know
how you could be happy all the years
without knowing
am I fine, or am I drinking wine
because I can't figure out the one thing
that's called life
at least I don't want to sound selfish
but my whole life plays without music
I love you
at all costs

Why are you so quiet

the storm breaks everything

the noise robs you of your dream

your thoughts are so loud

don't you even want to sleep

you don't dare to sleep

don't you even want to dream

you don't dare to take it in your own hand

your wishes

don't you wanna make a wish

you don't dare to socialize

not everyone wants to hurt you

and for me, you would never be replaceable

let's fall asleep arm in arm

and dream of our future

and tomorrow at 11:11

we pack our moving boxes

and go to the end for our wishes

I am asking myself
what keeps you up every night
It's the future
but you are safe in your dreams
because I take care of you
you don't know anything about all this
because my feelings for you
I will not reveal to you

I am asking myself
what keeps you up every night

You think you're nothing special

no matter how simple your outfit may look

I'm more than impressed by your eyes

you came sneaking up quietly like a snake

I haven't compared anything yet

but none could measure up to your purity

*You never stop loving someone
you just find a way
to trick your heart
and think you love someone else
or truly love someone
just because they are a look-a-like
and remind you of
your true love*

*I gave you my soul
my heart is yours
nothing is left
but I have no regrets*

You must forgive

if you want

that someone forgives you

It doesn't matter how long it lasts
it matters
how long it doesn't pass
how my love stays in your heart

You missed a lot of chances

while waiting for an answer

by someone who ghosted you

facit

don't waste your energy on others

you will need it

for yourself

We don't just break up

like other couples

we just have to deal with anxiety

we separate like twin flames

wrong time

we chose the wrong ways

just because it was easy

we think we don't deserve love

have to heal in separate

so we can shine in our golden hour

Let's be real
if I wanted someone
I could have someone
but I always wanted you
that's why I have no one

give people time
give them space
let them wander around
please nobody to stay
what is intended for you
will always be yours

I heard that you could die of loneliness
not that i feel sick
I feel nothing
I don't think of any disease
because I'm not a hypochondriac
I am just a dead individual that walks

We two could have stood against

the whole world

but we chose

to fight against each other

Sometimes you have to make a decision
that will break your heart into pieces
but will let your soul stay pure

True happiness is when we are

happy with ourselves

you need to love

yourself first

so someone else can

fall in love with you

Never ask question

you also don't want to be questioned

you know it will hurt you

even if you mean it nice

What I love the most about you

obviously, your soul

your eyes

your freckles

and your dimples

your remaining external features

are also nice to look

however

I don't stick to it

and you also shouldn't

everything is transient

and everything can also improve

I will not fight for you

because you can't fight for someone

you always lose

With you, it feels like a warm winter

without you can be the hottest summer day

a cold summer

I hope my eyes can hide the feelings inside
please call me back just for one minute
it's not because of me
it's not because I didn't say
everything
it's because my broken heart
wanna say goodbye
to the first and last love

It all began so easy

strangers

but it feels like

we have known each other for years

first Facetime call lasted seven hours

with you, infinity feels like

a ray of light

but where are we know

so much to say

but we stay so quite

it seems so easy to hurt each other

from lovers to strangers

just because we are

stubborn and afraid of love

Checking my phone
every second and hour
no messages that you've sent
I am still waiting for you
to come back for me and take
me wherever you wanna be

We can get to the moon

leave everything behind us

we don't need to waste our time

you like the cold time

and if it's important for you

we can travel to the coldest

place on Earth

it doesn't matter

because our love will keep us warm

We hurt each other so often

we were trapped in the dark

used to the loneliness

long forgotten what it means

togetherness, a foreign word for our vocabulary

We met in the park

everything was very relaxed

started sending us voice messages

it didn't last long

this resulted in hours of phone calls

without knowing it, we shared our secrets

our pain

our sorrow

just the two of us

but where are you now

everything divided

through a petty quarrel

In love since day one

thought I didn't deserve you

became cold and wary

I quickly lost myself in self-doubt

my life is shaped by the darkness

only when I met you

I learned to live

and not just to exist

little things that led to the dispute

became everyday life

everything went to your head

you drew the short line

our love suffered a short circuit

manifested the breakup

so to everyone

please stop

think positive

enjoy your happiness

if it meant to be it will last

if not

don't be sad

your twin flame is waiting

somewhere for you

You try to scare the shit out of me

found me in my new life

really thought I've been done with the hardest

part

why would someone does this to me

I tried to end it all

does it mean something to you

you stalked me

I just got one question

are you scared

how I can be happy

without you

you will never control me

again

And I was always there for you

but you don't call back in my hardest time

like you promise once

I still remember your words

clearly

I will go through it all

I want you by my side

I will go through our times

I will never leave you

I want to live my life with you

if you want it or not

I will be there for you

in your best and darkest time

How naive I could be
each of your promises began with a
I, like you, put myself first

I am over you
I am over us
if it was so easy
the hardest part is learning how to live without
you
but how could I survive
in a world without you
we build our small world
learned how it feels to be loved
now it's all destroyed

You promised me

and told me

I shouldn't forget

that you will love me forever

but forever never stays

I should know better

I'll be writing this song for the rest of my life

we broke up in the spring

since that day

winter has reigned in my heart

I can only embrace my memories

so that I don't freeze to death completely

You told me
now it's all over
the darkness is away
and the sunlight is awake
that I have you forever
who would have thought forever
could be severed
I've been sitting here for hours
I can't stop thinking
thinking about you
this wasn't what we planned for use
I gave you my heart
but it's still not enough

I never liked how I act

and maybe your love was just a joke

we were something different

when we were together

I told you I would never love someone more than

you

but now I am wiser

I will love us more

I was trapped on a boat

that never stops, just keeps pulling

straight into the darkness

I thought I belonged there

I thought it was my destiny

to be in the darkest room and never be loved

then you found my broken heart

on the ground

you took over the wheel

without any warning

I just learned how to love

you learned how it feels

to be loved

you threw an anchor overboard

and said

this was where I belonged

This is our story

I write it down

I can't stop thinking about you

I can't see you cry

when I know the tears belong to my wrong

decision

I will never hurt you anymore

I swear it to you and God

so I let you go

I see how you really are
I see how much pain you carry inside you
everyone lets you down

I try to understand you
try to look behind your facade
you don't see a way out
your last hope is a drug rush

if you only could see the true
if you knew how bleak my life is
if only you could see
how long the darkness has control
I don't know how to continue

How am I supposed to find my way through this

chaos on my own

you are drawn to the dark

you fight your grief by seeking protection from

false friends

you last chance out

alcohol

what should I say

I only want the best for you

I don't stress you with my problems

only want to help you

to bring you out of this shit situation

let it happen

let me show you a way out

my life is dark enough

yours doesn't have to be too

A snow falls in November

you want to live your whole life without me
you will always be there for me
in my downs and ups
you wish we met earlier
 how could I trust your words

how you have the dare to end it
when something doesn't go your way

I am over you
I try to fix my broken life
but stop
it comes all over me
the day we first meet
a snow falls in November
I am fine
I try to fix my broken heart
but stop
it all comes over me
the night we broke up for the second time

Now it's been a couple weeks ago

and you called me in the night

like nothing ever happened

you need me to fix it all

a day after, you call me again

you were so funny, kinda lovely and obviously
drunk

say you missed us

but I know in the morning

you will be gone

we can't be fixed and

we didn't have the harmony

it comes out of nowhere

it's funny, but drunk words are true words

so are you selfish or

are you still playing a game with me

Did you miss me just once

you know I always come back

didn't know my heart was so throughty

last night for the very first time

I was ready to end it all

but now I see it clearly

I can live without you

I don't want to play your game

I guess now you are

a single player

and you lost me forever

Only when we are pushed to our limits do we realize what we are capable of

You replaced me so easily
but you didn't see it
did you ?
you call your new love
you go out, and everything seems fine
you try to break me
making it official with her
but she doesn't reply
she hides you like a secret
at all cost

you found out
that I don't care about it
so you cheated on her
and started playing our game
with someone else

You replace me so easily
but we are not soulmates
we are twin flames
keep it in case
under all love letter
I send to you
the last words are always
I love you
you can try to replace the outside
but the inner will never fix
I never lose hope in the universe
it will keep pushing us together
our love can break any weather
and every dimension

Always be yourself

never try to be someone else

because in a world where

everyone tries to destroy yourself

you should stay strong

it will scare them

Others only see your appearance

so you assume that I also would

just admire your perfect figure

and see you as a trophy

you are wrong

the most beautiful thing about you

is what you can't see

but at the same time, hugs you warmly

the most beautiful visible thing

about you are your hazel eyes

where one breaks right into you, into your soul

untouchable, and yet I feel your love

even if you try to hide them with stubbornness

You want to show everyone your talent
but no one should know
that it's coming from you
our past defines how strong
we are in the present
our they don't define
our future

Your last name can

open doors for you

or it could be the hell

if you are named after someone

you hate

but you choose your future

Sometimes it takes one mistake

and everything is over

someone can make the same mistakes

over and over

and nothing happens

luck is in God's hands

don't push your luck

Just because someone move on

that doesn't mean

someone actually moved on

And again, it's me

who destroys everything

I'm afraid to lose you

I'm afraid you might leave me

my fear of loss restricts me

I can't breathe

I can't think

only way out

I push you further from me

just so you don't get a chance

to hurt me first

I'll take care of it

all by myself

I didn't know

a heart could sabotage itself

Sometimes you have

to grow separately

so that when you reconnect, we can shine

together

it's not about

the lost time or

what we couldn't do together

that doesn't bother us

it's about finding each other again

we heal ourselves

now it's time

for love

Now I am with somebody different,

but tell me why

I can't stop thinking

about your midnight green dress

I try so hard

to forget you

but the feelings for you

don't go away

To all the love songs
I never showed to you
to all the feelings
I never tell you
to all the stupid fights
keep it in mind
I love you

If I got a second chance

I would do it better

I keep writing you letters

I hope you're not mad now

but trust me when I say

I've changed

You say you hate me and that our story is over
I just replied, if it is hate
it is only the beginning
of a tragic love story

every separation hurt but if we stayed true to
ourselves
separation hurt but
After every separation we find more to ourselves
I can't wait for our union because that's our
destiny

I love you my dual soul
from your dual soul

I would like to show you how much
you mean to me
there is no time
in which I would not be reachable for you
there are no spatial boundaries
that I won't go for you
there is no law,
that I wouldn't break for you

I've had enough of listing words
I would like to prove to you with actions
what you mean to me
at first it was strange, why am I attracted to you
even though you trigger every cell in me

I've been thinking about us for nights
missed the time to sleep
and when I did
I only dreamed about you
your triggers led me to myself
Because when we first met
we were broken
had to trigger us to heal separately
as is usual for twinsflames